Beyond the Diagnosis: Finding Hope and Healing with Bipolar and Schizoaffective Disorder

Table of Contents

Introduction

Prologue

Part 1: **Understanding the Diagnoses**

Resources for Further Support

Acknowledgements

Introduction

This book is an invitation. It's a beacon of hope for those navigating the intricate landscapes of bipolar disorder or schizoaffective disorder. It's a testament to the resilience of the human spirit, a testament forged in the fires of personal experience. It's a journey of discovery, not just of these complex conditions, but of the strength, courage, and hope that reside within each of us.

I live with Bipolar Disorder (I also have Generalized Anxiety Disorder and Major Depressive Disorder). My son navigates the world with Schizoaffective Disorder. Together, we've weathered storms of mood swings, psychotic episodes, and the relentless challenges that these diagnoses bring. But we've also discovered profound truths about resilience, the power of connection, and the possibility of living a meaningful life beyond the labels.

This book is a continuation of my journey, a sequel to "Breaking Free," where I explored the terrain of anxiety and depression. Here, we delve deeper into the complexities of bipolar and schizoaffective disorder, offering a beacon of understanding, support, and hope to those who live with these conditions, their families, and anyone seeking to understand the intricacies of mental health.

We live in a world obsessed with labels. We categorize, define, and compartmentalize, seeking order in the chaos of human experience. But when it comes to mental health, labels can be both illuminating and limiting. They can offer a sense of understanding, a framework for making sense of our struggles. But they can also confine us, shaping our perceptions of ourselves and others, and casting shadows of stigma that are hard to escape.

Bipolar disorder and schizoaffective disorder are labels, diagnoses that describe a constellation of symptoms. But they are not the sum total of who we are. They are not our identities. They are not our destinies. They are simply a part of our stories, chapters in a larger narrative that is still being written.

Beyond the Labels

Bipolar disorder and schizoaffective disorder are often misunderstood, shrouded in stigma and misconception. They are painted as insurmountable obstacles, defining limitations rather than unique facets of human experience. But these diagnoses are not life sentences. They are not insurmountable barriers. They are part of a spectrum, a tapestry of human experience that encompasses both challenge and triumph.

In these pages, we will embark on a journey beyond the labels, beyond the confines of diagnosis. We will explore the intricate landscapes of bipolar and schizoaffective disorder, shedding light on their symptoms, their challenges, and their potential for healing and growth. We will share our personal stories, our struggles, and our triumphs, offering a hand of support and understanding to those who walk a similar path.

This is not a clinical textbook or a dry recitation of facts. It is a story of lived experience, a testament to the power of the human spirit to overcome adversity and find meaning in the midst of challenge. It is an invitation to join us on a journey of discovery, to explore the depths of these conditions, and to emerge with a renewed sense of hope and possibility.

This book is a testament to that belief. It is a message of hope for those who feel lost, alone, or overwhelmed by their diagnosis. It is a reminder that you are not alone, that there is support available, and that you have the strength within you to navigate this journey and create a life filled with meaning and purpose.

Join us as we embark on this journey together, a journey beyond the diagnosis, a journey of hope, healing, and possibility.

Prologue

Our Journey, Your Journey

My journey with bipolar disorder began in the shadows, a whisper of instability that gradually grew into a roar. The highs were exhilarating, a surge of energy and creativity that propelled me forward. But the lows were devastating, a crushing weight of despair that threatened to consume me.

For my son, schizoaffective disorder manifested as a confusing blend of mood swings and psychotic episodes. The world became a distorted kaleidoscope of hallucinations and delusions, a terrifying labyrinth where reality blurred with the unreal.

Together, we've navigated these challenges, learning to recognize the signs, to manage the symptoms, and to find moments of peace amidst the chaos. We've discovered the power of medication, therapy, and lifestyle changes, but most importantly, we've found strength in each other, in our shared experience, and in the support of our family and friends.

This book is an offering of our journey, our lessons learned, and our belief in the possibility of healing and growth. It is an invitation to join us as we explore the complexities of bipolar and schizoaffective disorder, offering a roadmap for navigating these challenging terrains and finding hope in the midst of adversity.

A Message of Hope

Living with bipolar disorder or schizoaffective disorder is not easy. It is a journey filled with ups and downs, with moments of clarity and moments of confusion. But it is also a journey of profound strength, resilience, and hope.

We believe that it is possible to live a meaningful life with these diagnoses. It is possible to find joy, to pursue passions, and to build fulfilling relationships. It is possible to manage symptoms, to find stability, and to embrace the unique tapestry of your own experience.

This book is about moving beyond the labels, beyond the diagnoses, and embracing the fullness of our humanity. It's about recognizing that while these conditions present unique challenges, they also offer opportunities for growth, resilience, and a deeper understanding of ourselves and the world around us.

We will explore the science behind these disorders, shedding light on the intricate workings of the brain and the complex interplay of genetics, environment, and life experiences. We will delve into the lived experience of bipolar and schizoaffective disorder, sharing personal stories of triumphs and setbacks, of hope and despair, of finding strength in the face of adversity.

But most importantly, we will offer a message of hope. We will share strategies for managing symptoms, for coping with challenges, and for building a life filled with meaning and purpose. We will celebrate the resilience of the human spirit and the power of connection, reminding you that you are not alone on this journey.

This book is for you if you are living with bipolar or schizoaffective disorder, seeking to understand your experiences and find ways to thrive. It's for your loved ones, who want to support you with compassion and understanding. And it's for anyone who wants to learn more about mental health, challenge stigma, and embrace the diversity of human experience.

Together, let's embark on a journey beyond the diagnosis, a journey toward hope, healing, and a life filled with meaning and purpose.

Part 1: Understanding the Diagnoses

Chapter 1

Two Journeys, One Path: Schizoaffective and Bipolar Disorder

September 2018. The buzz of the office faded as I stared at my phone, utterly bewildered. A message from my son, a map with a pin dropped near a hospital I vaguely recognized. "The car is in the garage by that hospital on the map," it read. Confusion swirled within me. He'd mentioned going to the doctor earlier, not feeling well, but this... this was unexpected. A knot of worry tightened in my chest and full blown anxiety took over. This was when my anxiety exacerbated marking the start of a long and treacherous journey.

Hours later, the word "schizophrenia" echoed in the sterile hospital room. The doctor explained, but the term seemed to hang in the air, heavy and unfamiliar. My son, usually so vibrant, was just lost in a world I couldn't reach. Days of hospital visits, medications, whispered conversations with doctors, and a gnawing fear I tried to keep hidden from my son.

When he finally came home, it was a fragile homecoming. I waited, not wanting to push, for him to tell me what was happening in his own time. Slowly, the pieces began to fall into place. "I hear voices, Mom," he confessed one day, his voice barely a whisper. "I've been hearing them since I was a child."

Something had shifted, something had intensified those voices, turning his world into a confusing, frightening place. He'd pace the house, asking if I'd called him, if I'd said something when I hadn't. Then there was the night I woke with a jolt, a mother's intuition screaming that something was wrong. Downstairs, in the middle of winter, he sat on the front step, shivering in shorts and a thin vest, our dog huddled in his lap. "The neighbor is dying, Mom," he said, his eyes wide with panic. "We need to call an ambulance."

I looked out at the quiet street, the houses dark and still. There was no ambulance, no dying neighbor, just the chilling reality of his altered perception. Gently, I coaxed him back inside, reassuring him, and trying to soothe the fear that gripped us both.

The hospital stay provided some answers, but even more questions lingered.   After months of questions we found ourselves in the office of a psychiatrist, a specialist who could hopefully shed more light on what my son was experiencing. After what felt like endless questioning and tests, the diagnosis came: Schizoaffective Disorder, Bipolar Type.

Schizoaffective Disorder... even the name felt like a mouthful, a jumble of syllables I could barely pronounce. Bipolar Type... What did that even mean? I'd heard of bipolar disorder, of course, but this was something entirely different, something I'd never encountered before. The weight of this unfamiliar diagnosis pressed down on me, a mix of fear and determination swirling within. I had to understand. I had to learn how to help my son navigate this new and challenging terrain.

Even before the pandemic, the stress of my son's illness took a toll on my own mental health. My anxiety and depression worsened, a constant undercurrent that threatened to overwhelm me. Then, the pandemic hit, adding an extra layer of isolation, uncertainty, and fear. I struggled to navigate the new reality, to find a balance between caring for my son, protecting myself, and coping with my own mental health challenges.

The Unseen Current: My Undiagnosed Bipolar

Looking back, the signs were there, subtle whispers of something amiss long before my son's diagnosis. I'd always been intense, my emotions running a little deeper, a little higher, than those around me. But I chalked it up to personality, to being "sensitive" or "passionate."

There were periods of restless energy, when sleep felt like a waste of precious time. Ideas would race through my mind, a whirlwind of creativity and ambition. My enthusiasm boundless, my confidence unshakeable. These bursts of productivity and seemingly limitless energy were often followed by crashes, days or weeks when I could barely drag myself out of bed. The world would turn gray, joy a distant memory, and even the simplest tasks felt insurmountable.

I dismissed these fluctuations as the normal ups and downs of life, the inevitable consequences of stress and a busy schedule. I didn't recognize them as the telltale signs of bipolar disorder, a condition that would later become a central part of my story.

Feeling Misunderstood and Out of Place

The isolation was profound. I felt like an alien, observing the world from a distance, unable to connect with the people around me. Friends and family would tell me I was acting weird, that I was strange, but I didn't understand what they meant. I thought I was behaving normally, that everyone felt the same way, just to a lesser degree.

The disconnect deepened as I lost relationships and friendships. People started pulling away, their discomfort with my behavior palpable. I felt like a leper, ostracized for a condition I didn't even understand. Someone even asked me once, "Is there anything that could make you happy?" I stared at them, blankly, unsure how to answer.

My therapist had been observing my struggles. She'd seen the highs and lows, the shifts in my energy and mood. One day, during a particularly vulnerable session, I opened up completely. I poured out my heart, sharing my fears, my anxieties, the overwhelming sense of disconnection, and the impulsive desires that often took hold.

When I finally finished, a wave of relief washed over me. Then, my therapist spoke, her voice gentle but firm. "You're showing signs and symptoms of Bipolar Disorder," she said. "I think you should see your psychiatrist."

The word hung in the air – Bipolar Disorder. It wasn't entirely unfamiliar, but I'd never considered it as a possibility for myself. Fear mingled with a strange sense of validation. Could this be the explanation for the internal chaos I'd been battling for so long?

The psychiatrist's office was a place of stark contrasts – sterile and clinical, yet filled with the weight of human emotion. Questionnaires, evaluations, and a deep dive into my personal history followed. Finally, the diagnosis was confirmed: Bipolar Disorder.

Relief warred with apprehension. A label, a definition, a framework for understanding the turbulence within me. But also, a new set of challenges, a lifelong journey of management and self-discovery.

My son's diagnosis with Schizoaffective Disorder, Bipolar Type, was a shock, a plunge into the unknown. But amidst the fear and confusion, there was also a strange sense of familiarity. The psychiatrist's words echoed in my mind: "Bipolar Type." Suddenly, my own recent diagnosis with Bipolar Disorder wasn't just a personal struggle; it was a thread connecting me to my son, a shared experience in a new and unexpected way.

We were both navigating the choppy waters of mental illness, each with our own unique challenges. But we were in this together, two individuals bound by a shared understanding, a shared determination to find a way forward.

And this is where I want to be clear: while diagnoses provide a framework, a language to understand what we're experiencing, they are not the whole story. They don't define us. My son is not his Schizoaffective Disorder, just as I am not my Bipolar Disorder. We are individuals with strengths, passions, and dreams that exist beyond the labels.

This is crucial to remember, not just for ourselves, but for how we approach others with mental health conditions. We must see beyond the diagnoses, beyond the symptoms, and recognize the unique personhood of each individual. It's about fostering empathy, compassion, and a willingness to truly understand the human experience behind the labels.

Chapter 2

Unveiling Schizoaffective Disorder

In the previous chapter, we explored our personal journey with bipolar disorder and schizoaffective disorder. We now shift our focus to schizoaffective disorder, the complex condition that my son lives with. This chapter aims to provide a comprehensive overview of schizoaffective disorder, including its defining characteristics, symptom spectrum, and available treatment options. While the focus will be on the bipolar type, which affects my son, we will also touch upon the depressive type to provide a complete picture of this often-misunderstood illness.

Schizoaffective disorder is a chronic mental health condition that involves a combination of psychotic symptoms and mood symptoms. It's like a blend of schizophrenia and a mood disorder, such as bipolar disorder or depression.

Key Features:

Psychotic symptoms: These include hallucinations (seeing or hearing things that aren't there), delusions (false beliefs), disorganized thinking, and abnormal motor behavior.

Mood symptoms: These can include periods of mania (elevated mood, increased energy, racing thoughts) or depression (low mood, loss of interest, fatigue).

Schizoaffective disorder is **not** simply having schizophrenia and a mood disorder at the same time. It's a distinct diagnosis with its own unique set of challenges. The symptoms can vary greatly from person to person, making it a highly individualized experience. While it's a chronic condition, effective treatment can help people manage their symptoms and live fulfilling lives.

Think of it this way:

Imagine a Venn diagram with two overlapping circles. One circle represents schizophrenia, with its psychotic symptoms. The other circle represents mood disorders, with their mood-related symptoms. Schizoaffective disorder sits in the overlapping area, where both sets of symptoms are present.

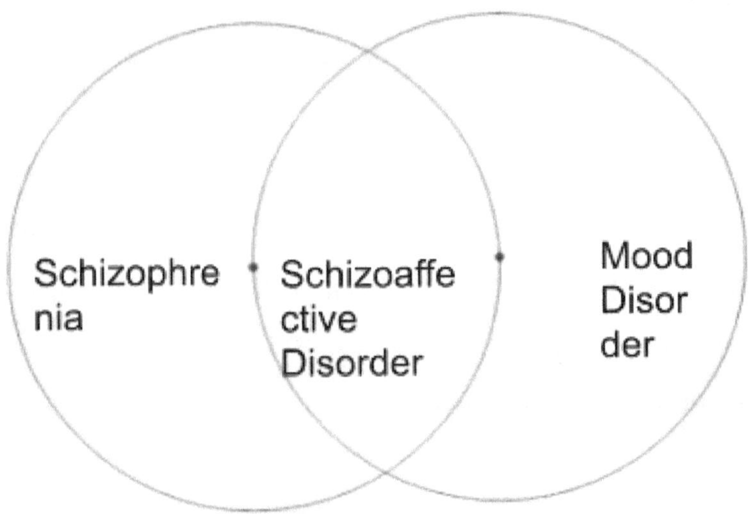

This definition and diagram provides a clear and concise explanation of schizoaffective disorder, setting the stage for a deeper exploration of its symptoms and impact in the rest of the chapter.

Schizoaffective disorder presents a unique set of challenges due to the presence of psychosis, which can manifest in the form of hallucinations and delusions. These symptoms can significantly disrupt a person's perception of reality, making it difficult to distinguish between what is real and what is not.

Hallucinations:

Sensory experiences that are not real: Hallucinations can involve any of the five senses. Auditory hallucinations (hearing voices) are the most common, but visual hallucinations (seeing things), olfactory hallucinations (smelling things), tactile hallucinations (feeling sensations on the skin), and gustatory hallucinations (tasting things) can also occur.

Distressing and disruptive: Hallucinations can be very distressing and can interfere with daily life. They can make it difficult to concentrate, hold a conversation, or perform tasks. They can also lead to social isolation and withdrawal.

Imagine constantly hearing voices whispering criticisms or commands. This can be incredibly distracting and anxiety-provoking, making it difficult to focus on work, school, or relationships.

Delusions:

False beliefs that are firmly held despite evidence to the contrary: Delusions can take many forms, such as delusions of grandeur (believing you have special powers or abilities), delusions of persecution (believing that others are trying to harm you), or delusions of reference (believing that everyday events have special meaning or significance).

Impact on behavior and decision-making: Delusions can influence a person's behavior and decision-making. They can lead to paranoia, social isolation, and even dangerous actions.

Challenges of living with psychosis:

- Difficulty distinguishing reality: Psychosis can make it extremely difficult to determine what is real and what is not, leading to confusion, fear, and anxiety.

- Impaired functioning: Psychosis can interfere with daily functioning, making it challenging to maintain relationships, hold a job, or take care of basic needs.

- Stigma and social isolation: People with psychosis often face stigma and discrimination, which can lead to social isolation and feelings of shame.

Coping and support:

Medication: Antipsychotic medications can help reduce the severity of hallucinations and delusions.

Therapy: Cognitive-behavioral therapy (CBT) can help individuals learn to identify and challenge their psychotic symptoms.

Social support: Having a strong support system of family, friends, and mental health professionals can make a significant difference in managing psychosis.

It's important to remember that people with schizoaffective disorder can lead fulfilling lives with the right treatment and support. By understanding the challenges of psychosis, we can foster empathy and compassion for those who experience it.

Schizoaffective disorder presents a unique set of challenges due to its complex interplay of psychotic and mood symptoms. These challenges can significantly impact various aspects of an individual's life, including:

Diagnostic Challenges:

Overlapping Symptoms: Schizoaffective disorder shares symptoms with both schizophrenia and mood disorders, making it difficult to diagnose accurately. It can be mistaken for either condition, leading to delays in appropriate treatment.

Fluctuating Symptoms: The symptoms of schizoaffective disorder can fluctuate over time, with periods of relative stability interspersed with episodes of acute psychosis or mood disturbance. This variability can make it challenging to establish a consistent treatment plan.

Functional Challenges:

Cognitive Impairment: Schizoaffective disorder can affect cognitive functions such as attention, memory, and executive functioning, making it difficult to concentrate, learn, and make decisions. This can impact academic or occupational performance and daily tasks.

Social Isolation: The combination of psychotic and mood symptoms can lead to social withdrawal and isolation.

Individuals may struggle with interpersonal relationships due to paranoia, disorganized thinking, or mood instability.

Daily Living Skills: Difficulties with motivation, organization, and decision-making can make it challenging to manage daily tasks such as cooking, cleaning, and personal hygiene.

Treatment Challenges:

Medication Management: Finding the right combination of medications to manage both psychotic and mood symptoms can be complex and require ongoing adjustments.

Treatment Adherence: Individuals with schizoaffective disorder may struggle to adhere to their treatment plan due to side effects, lack of insight into their illness, or difficulties with motivation and organization.

Importance of Early Intervention

Early intervention in schizoaffective disorder is crucial for several reasons:

- **Improved Prognosis:** Early diagnosis and treatment can lead to better long-term outcomes, reducing the severity and frequency of episodes and improving overall functioning.

- **Minimizing Functional Decline:** Early intervention can help prevent or minimize the functional decline associated with the illness, allowing individuals to maintain their independence and achieve their goals.

- **Reducing Relapse Risk:** Starting treatment early and adhering to it can significantly reduce the risk of relapse and hospitalization.

- **Enhancing Quality of Life:** Early intervention can help individuals manage their symptoms, cope with challenges, and improve their overall quality of life.

Differentiating Schizoaffective Disorder from Schizophrenia and Bipolar Disorder

It's important to distinguish schizoaffective disorder from both schizophrenia and bipolar disorder, as they share some overlapping symptoms but have key differences.

Schizophrenia

Primarily characterized by psychosis: The hallmark of schizophrenia is persistent psychosis, including hallucinations, delusions, disorganized thinking, and negative symptoms (e.g., flat affect, social withdrawal).

Mood symptoms may occur, but are less prominent: While individuals with schizophrenia may experience mood disturbances, these are typically secondary to the psychotic symptoms and not as severe or prolonged as in schizoaffective disorder.

Focus on managing psychosis: Treatment primarily focuses on managing psychotic symptoms with antipsychotic medications and therapy.

Bipolar Disorder

Characterized by significant mood swings: The defining feature of bipolar disorder is distinct episodes of mania and depression, with periods of relatively normal mood in between.

Psychotic symptoms may occur during mood episodes: Some individuals with bipolar disorder may experience psychotic symptoms, but these typically only occur during manic or depressive episodes and resolve with mood stabilizers.

Focus on mood stabilization: Treatment focuses on stabilizing mood with mood stabilizers, antidepressants, and therapy.

Schizoaffective Disorder

Combines features of both: Schizoaffective disorder involves both persistent psychosis and prominent mood episodes.

Psychotic symptoms persist even when mood is stable: Unlike bipolar disorder, where psychotic symptoms are typically tied to mood episodes, in schizoaffective disorder, psychosis continues even when mood is relatively stable.

Treatment addresses both psychosis and mood: Treatment involves a combination of antipsychotic medications, mood stabilizers, and therapy to address both the psychotic and mood symptoms.

By understanding these distinctions, you can better appreciate the unique challenges of schizoaffective disorder and the need for tailored treatment approaches.

Schizoaffective disorder requires a comprehensive treatment approach that addresses both psychotic and mood symptoms. Medication, psychotherapy, and lifestyle changes are the mainstays of treatment. Early intervention and ongoing treatment are crucial for managing symptoms, preventing relapse, and improving quality of life.

It's important to remember that treatment is highly individualized and should be tailored to the specific needs of each person with schizoaffective disorder. By working closely with a mental health professional, individuals can develop a treatment plan that helps them achieve their goals and live a fulfilling life.

Chapter 3

Unmasking Bipolar Disorder

Bipolar disorder is a mental health condition that causes significant shifts in a person's mood, energy levels, and ability to function. Imagine a rollercoaster with extreme highs and lows – that's a way to visualize the experience of bipolar disorder. These shifts can be dramatic and unpredictable, making it challenging to navigate daily life.

The Highs and Lows

People with bipolar disorder experience periods of intense emotions, both "highs" and "lows."

- **Mania or Hypomania (the highs):** During these periods, a person might feel incredibly happy, energetic, and even euphoric. They might have racing thoughts, talk rapidly, sleep less, and engage in impulsive behaviors. While mania can feel good at first, it can also lead to poor judgment, risky decisions, and even psychosis (a break from reality). Hypomania is a less severe form of mania.

- **Depression (the lows):** These periods are characterized by deep sadness, hopelessness, loss of interest in activities, fatigue, and difficulty concentrating. People experiencing a depressive episode might also have changes in appetite and sleep, and thoughts of self-harm or suicide.

It's More Than Just Mood Swings

It's important to understand that bipolar disorder is more than just ordinary mood swings. The mood changes are more extreme, last longer, and significantly impact a person's life, relationships, and work.

Different Types of Bipolar Disorder

There are different types of bipolar disorder, including:

Bipolar I: Characterized by at least one manic episode, often with depressive episodes as well. This is the classic presentation of bipolar disorder. It involves experiencing at least one manic episode, which can be so intense it may require hospitalization. Depressive episodes are common in Bipolar I, but not always required for a diagnosis.

Bipolar II: In this type, a person experiences hypomania, a milder form of mania. While hypomania might increase energy and productivity, it doesn't generally lead to the severe impairment caused by full-blown mania. However, people with Bipolar II experience periods of major depression that can be just as debilitating as those in Bipolar I.

Cyclothymic Disorder: This is a milder form of bipolar disorder characterized by frequent shifts between hypomania and mild depression. These mood swings are less extreme than in Bipolar I or II, but they persist for at least two years, causing significant disruption to a person's life.

Recognizing the Symptoms

The symptoms of bipolar disorder can vary widely from person to person. It's important to remember that not everyone will experience every symptom, and the intensity can change over time.

Symptoms of Mania and Hypomania:

Elevated mood: Feeling excessively happy, euphoric, or "high."

Increased energy: Having boundless energy, needing little sleep, and feeling restless.

Racing thoughts: Experiencing a rapid flow of ideas and difficulty concentrating.

Increased talkativeness: Speaking rapidly, jumping between topics, and feeling pressured to keep talking.

Inflated self-esteem: Having an exaggerated sense of self-importance or grandiosity.

Impulsivity: Engaging in risky behaviors, such as spending sprees, reckless driving, or substance abuse.

Decreased need for sleep: Feeling like you don't need sleep and can function on very little.

Irritability and agitation: Feeling easily annoyed or frustrated.

Symptoms of Depression:

Depressed mood: Feeling sad, hopeless, empty, or tearful.

Loss of interest: Losing interest in activities that were once enjoyable.

Fatigue: Feeling tired, sluggish, and lacking in energy.

Changes in sleep: Sleeping too much or too little.

Changes in appetite: Eating more or less than usual.

Difficulty concentrating: Having trouble focusing, remembering things, or making decisions.

Feelings of worthlessness or guilt: Feeling excessively guilty or like a failure.

Thoughts of death or suicide: Having recurring thoughts of death, self-harm, or suicide.

Important Note: If you or someone you know is experiencing thoughts of self-harm or suicide, please seek help immediately. You can call the 988 Suicide & Crisis Lifeline (or visit 988lifeline.org) for confidential support.

The symptoms of bipolar disorder can vary widely. Not everyone will experience every symptom, and the intensity can change over time. Here's a breakdown of common symptoms associated with mania/hypomania and depression:

Mania/Hypomania	Depression
Mood	**Mood**
Excessively happy, euphoric, or "high"	Sad, hopeless, empty, or tearful
Irritable, agitated, or easily angered	-
Energy & Activity	**Energy & Activity**
Increased energy, restlessness	Fatigue, lack of energy
Decreased need for sleep	Sleeping too much or too little
Increased activity, racing thoughts	Slowed movements,

	difficulty concentrating
Thinking & Behavior	**Thinking & Behavior**
Rapid speech, jumping between topics	-
Inflated self-esteem, grandiosity	Feelings of worthlessness or guilt
Impulsivity, risky behaviors	-
Physical Symptoms	**Physical Symptoms**
-	Changes in appetite (eating more or less)

Beyond the Myths: Confronting Misconceptions and Stigma

Bipolar disorder is often misunderstood, and harmful stereotypes can create barriers to diagnosis, treatment, and recovery. Let's debunk some common misconceptions:

Myth 1: "People with bipolar disorder are just moody."

Reality: Bipolar disorder is far more than typical mood swings. The mood shifts are extreme, long-lasting, and significantly disrupt daily life, relationships, and work. While everyone experiences fluctuations in mood, bipolar disorder involves distinct episodes of mania or hypomania and depression that are far more intense and disruptive than everyday emotions.

Myth 2: "Bipolar disorder is all about mania."

Reality: While mania is a defining feature of bipolar I disorder, the depressive episodes are often more frequent and can be just as debilitating. Bipolar II disorder involves hypomania and depression, and cyclothymic disorder involves less severe but persistent mood swings. Focusing solely on mania ignores the significant impact of depression in bipolar disorder.

Myth 3: "People with bipolar disorder are dangerous or violent."

Reality: This is a harmful stereotype. The vast majority of people with bipolar disorder are not violent. Like anyone else, they may experience irritability or anger, especially during mood episodes, but they are no more likely to be violent than the general population. Stigma and discrimination can actually worsen symptoms and create barriers to getting help.

Myth 4: "Bipolar disorder means you can't have a successful life."

Reality: With proper treatment and support, people with bipolar disorder can lead fulfilling and productive lives. Many individuals successfully manage their condition and achieve their goals in relationships, careers, and personal pursuits.

Myth 5: "People with bipolar disorder are unpredictable and unreliable."

Reality: While mood episodes can be unpredictable, with treatment and self-management strategies, many people with bipolar disorder can maintain stability and lead reliable lives. It's important to remember that bipolar disorder is a medical condition, not a character flaw.

Breaking the Stigma

Stigma thrives on silence and misinformation. By talking openly about bipolar disorder, educating ourselves and others, and challenging stereotypes, we can help break down the stigma and create a more supportive environment for those living with this condition.

It's time to move beyond fear and judgment and embrace understanding and compassion. Each of us has a role to play in creating a more supportive world for those affected by bipolar disorder.

Challenging stigma is not just about changing attitudes; it's about saving lives. By raising awareness, promoting understanding, and advocating for change, we can create a world where everyone affected by bipolar disorder feels supported, empowered, and hopeful.

Become an Advocate for Change

Here are ways you can make a difference:

Start the conversation: Talk openly about mental health with your friends, family, and colleagues. Share your own experiences if you feel comfortable, or simply express your support for those living with mental health conditions.

Educate yourself and others: Learn more about bipolar disorder and other mental illnesses. Share accurate information with those around you and challenge misconceptions when you encounter them.

Support mental health organizations: Donate to or volunteer with organizations like NAMI (National Alliance on Mental Illness) or DBSA (Depression and Bipolar Support Alliance) that provide resources and support to individuals and families affected by mental illness.

Advocate for change in your community: Encourage schools, workplaces, and community organizations to create mental health-friendly environments and promote mental wellness.

Share your story (if you feel comfortable): Sharing your personal experiences with mental illness can be incredibly powerful in reducing stigma and inspiring others.

Support legislation that promotes mental health: Contact your elected officials to express your support for policies that improve access to mental health care and support services.

My Journey with Bipolar Disorder

My journey with bipolar disorder began in January 2023, though I didn't know it at the time. I was already seeking help for anxiety and depression, attending therapy sessions weekly. It was actually my therapist who first recognized the patterns of bipolar disorder in my behavior and emotions. She alerted my psychiatrist, who then conducted a thorough assessment and confirmed the diagnosis.

Looking back, the signs were there, but I had simply thought that everyone experienced such intense highs and lows. I'd have weeks of crushing depression that lingered even after happy events, followed by periods of inexplicable euphoria. I now understand those shifting moods were not just "me" but symptoms of an underlying condition.

There were times I acted recklessly, making decisions that left me questioning my own judgment. *What did you do? This isn't you!* I'd often think to myself. The diagnosis finally provided an explanation for those out-of-character moments.

Finding the right medication was a process of trial and error. My initial prescription made me so ill that my psychiatrist had to adjust it several times before we found a combination that worked for me. This experience taught me the importance of patience, self-advocacy, and open communication with my healthcare providers.

While there's no cure for bipolar disorder, I've learned to accept it as a treatable condition. I'm living proof that you can have a fulfilling life with this diagnosis. I have a career, loving relationships, and I pursue my passions. It's not always easy, and I sometimes struggle with self-consciousness and the lingering stigma surrounding mental illness. But I remind myself that bipolar disorder is a medical condition, not a character flaw.

I'm fortunate to have a strong support system. My close friends and family understand my diagnosis and accept me for who I am. Sadly, not everyone has been so understanding. Some people disappeared from my life after I opened up about my diagnosis, which was painful. But it also showed me the importance of surrounding myself with people who truly care and support me.

Bipolar disorder is not a life sentence. It's a condition that can be managed, and people who live with it deserve understanding and compassion. By sharing my story, I hope to challenge misconceptions and encourage others to seek help and support. Together, we can create a world where mental health is openly discussed, and everyone feels empowered to live their best life, regardless of their diagnosis. Living with bipolar disorder can be challenging, but it's important to remember that it is a treatable condition. With the right combination of medication, therapy, and lifestyle changes, people with bipolar disorder can lead fulfilling and meaningful lives.

Chapter 4

The Intersection of Bipolar and Schizoaffective Disorders

While bipolar disorder and schizoaffective disorder are distinct conditions, they share some overlapping symptoms, which can make diagnosis and treatment more challenging. For individuals with a dual diagnosis, or for their loved ones, understanding these complexities is crucial for navigating the path toward recovery and well-being.

Unique Challenges for Individuals with a Dual Diagnosis

Diagnostic Challenges: The overlapping symptoms of mood swings and psychosis can make it difficult to distinguish between bipolar disorder with psychotic features and schizoaffective disorder. Accurate diagnosis is essential for developing an effective treatment plan.

Treatment Complexity: Managing both conditions often requires a combination of medications, therapies, and lifestyle adjustments. Finding the right balance of treatments can be a process of trial and error, requiring close collaboration with mental health professionals.

Increased Symptom Burden: Individuals with a dual diagnosis may experience a wider range of symptoms, including mood swings, psychosis, depression, anxiety, and cognitive difficulties. This can significantly impact daily functioning and quality of life.

Higher Risk of Complications: A dual diagnosis may increase the risk of substance abuse, suicide attempts, and hospitalization. It's crucial to address these risks proactively and have a strong support system in place.

Social and Occupational Challenges: The symptoms of both conditions can make it challenging to maintain stable relationships, employment, and social connections. Support and understanding from loved ones and employers are essential.

Challenges for Loved Ones

Understanding the Conditions: It can be difficult for loved ones to understand the complexities of both diagnoses and how they interact. Education and support groups can be invaluable resources.

Communication and Support: Individuals with a dual diagnosis may experience difficulties with communication and emotional regulation. Loved ones need to develop effective communication strategies and provide consistent emotional support.

Setting Boundaries: It's important for loved ones to establish healthy boundaries while still providing support. This can be challenging, especially during periods of crisis.

Caregiver Burnout: Caring for someone with a dual diagnosis can be emotionally and physically demanding. Loved ones need to prioritize their own well-being and seek support when needed.

Finding Hope and Support

Despite the challenges, it's important to remember that recovery is possible. With the right treatment, support, and self-care strategies, individuals with a dual diagnosis can lead fulfilling lives.

Seek professional help: A qualified mental health professional can provide accurate diagnosis, develop a personalized treatment plan, and offer ongoing support.

Build a strong support system: Connect with friends, family, or support groups for emotional support and encouragement.

Prioritize self-care: Engage in activities that promote physical and mental well-being, such as exercise, healthy eating, relaxation techniques, and hobbies.

Educate yourself: Learn as much as you can about both conditions and available treatment options.

Advocate for your needs: Don't be afraid to speak up for yourself and seek the support you need.

The Ripple Effect: How Bipolar and Schizoaffective Disorders Impact Family Dynamics

Living with bipolar disorder or schizoaffective disorder, or loving someone who does, inevitably impacts family dynamics and relationships. The unpredictable nature of these conditions, coupled with the emotional intensity of mood swings and potential psychotic episodes, can strain even the strongest bonds.

Challenges Within the Family System

Emotional Rollercoaster: Family members often find themselves on an emotional rollercoaster, mirroring the ups and downs of their loved one's condition. This can lead to feelings of exhaustion, anxiety, and even resentment.

Communication Breakdowns: During mood episodes, communication can become challenging. Mania might lead to rapid speech and racing thoughts that are difficult to follow, while depression might result in withdrawal and silence.

Shifting Roles and Responsibilities: As the individual with the diagnosis navigates their condition, family roles may shift. Someone might take on more caregiving responsibilities, impacting their own work, relationships, and well-being.

Fear and Worry: Loved ones often experience constant worry about the individual's safety and well-being, especially during periods of crisis or when suicidal thoughts are present.

Financial Strain: The costs associated with treatment, medication, and potential loss of income due to the condition can create financial stress for the entire family.

Social Isolation: Families may withdraw from social activities due to the unpredictable nature of the conditions or the stigma associated with mental illness.

Impact on Relationships

Strain on Intimate Relationships: The emotional intensity and unpredictable behavior associated with bipolar and schizoaffective disorders can put a significant strain on romantic relationships. Partners may struggle with feelings of confusion, frustration, and helplessness.

Challenges in Parenting: Parents with these conditions may face difficulties providing consistent care and emotional support to their children. It's essential for them to seek support and develop coping strategies to navigate parenting challenges.

Impact on Friendships: Maintaining friendships can be challenging. Friends may struggle to understand the condition and its impact, leading to misunderstandings or withdrawal.

Navigating the Challenges

Open Communication: Honest and open communication is crucial. Family members need to express their feelings, concerns, and needs in a supportive and constructive way.

Education: Learning about bipolar and schizoaffective disorders can help family members understand the conditions, recognize symptoms, and develop effective coping strategies.

Boundaries: Setting healthy boundaries is essential for both the individual with the diagnosis and their loved ones. This helps protect everyone's emotional well-being and prevents resentment.

Support Groups: Connecting with other families who are going through similar experiences can provide invaluable support, understanding, and practical advice.

Family Therapy: Family therapy can help improve communication, resolve conflicts, and strengthen relationships.

Self-Care: It's crucial for family members to prioritize their own well-being. This includes engaging in self-care activities, seeking support when needed, and setting realistic expectations.

While bipolar and schizoaffective disorders present significant challenges for families, they don't have to define family relationships. With understanding, communication, and support, families can navigate these challenges and build stronger, more resilient bonds.

Navigating the Treatment Maze: Finding the Right Balance

When it comes to treating bipolar disorder and schizoaffective disorder, especially when they occur together, finding the right balance of medications, therapies, and lifestyle adjustments is crucial. It's rarely a one-size-fits-all approach, and the journey often involves careful monitoring, open communication, and a willingness to adapt.

The Complexity of Medication Management

Multiple Medications: Individuals with a dual diagnosis may require a combination of medications to address both mood swings and psychotic symptoms. This can involve mood stabilizers, antipsychotics, antidepressants, and possibly anxiety medications.

Side Effects: Managing potential side effects from multiple medications can be challenging. It requires close monitoring and open communication with the prescribing physician.

Medication Interactions: It's essential to be aware of potential interactions between different medications.

Finding the Right Dosage: Determining the optimal dosage for each medication often requires careful titration and adjustments over time.

The Role of Therapy

Addressing Both Conditions: Therapy plays a vital role in helping individuals understand and manage both bipolar and schizoaffective disorder. It provides coping strategies for mood swings, psychotic symptoms, and the challenges of daily life.

Different Therapeutic Approaches: Various therapy modalities can be helpful, including Cognitive Behavioral Therapy (CBT), Interpersonal and Social Rhythm Therapy (IPSRT), and family-focused therapy.

Building a Therapeutic Alliance: A strong therapeutic relationship with a trusted mental health professional is essential for navigating the complexities of treatment.

The Importance of Lifestyle Factors

Routine and Stability: Maintaining a regular routine, including consistent sleep patterns, healthy eating habits, and regular exercise, can significantly impact mood stability and overall well-being.

Stress Management: Learning effective stress management techniques, such as mindfulness, meditation, or yoga, can help reduce the frequency and intensity of mood episodes.

Substance Abuse: It's crucial to avoid alcohol and drugs, as they can worsen symptoms and interfere with medication effectiveness.

Social Support: A strong support network of friends, family, or support groups can provide emotional support and encouragement throughout the treatment journey.

Finding the Right Balance: An Ongoing Process

Finding the right treatment balance is often an ongoing process that requires patience, persistence, and a willingness to adapt. It's important to:

Work Closely with Professionals: Collaborate closely with your psychiatrist, therapist, and other healthcare providers to develop a personalized treatment plan.

Monitor Symptoms and Side Effects: Keep track of your symptoms, medication side effects, and any changes in your overall well-being.

Communicate Openly: Don't hesitate to discuss any concerns or questions with your healthcare team.

Be Patient and Persistent: Finding the right balance takes time. Don't get discouraged if adjustments are needed along the way.

Chapter 5

The Interplay of Genes and Environment

Genetics and family history

It's important to understand that both bipolar disorder and schizoaffective disorder are complex conditions with no single cause. Genetics and family history play a significant role, but they are intertwined with environmental factors. Here's a breakdown of how these elements contribute to each disorder:

Bipolar Disorder

Heritability: Bipolar disorder is highly heritable, meaning a large portion of the risk comes from genes passed down in families. Studies suggest that if one identical twin has bipolar disorder, the other twin has a 40-70% chance of also developing it. This is much higher than the risk for fraternal twins or siblings, highlighting the genetic influence.

Specific Genes: While no single "bipolar gene" exists, research has identified several genes that may increase susceptibility. These include genes involved in brain signaling, neurotransmitter regulation, and stress response.

Family History: Having a close relative (parent, sibling, child) with bipolar disorder significantly increases your risk. The closer the relative and the more relatives affected, the higher the risk.

Schizoaffective Disorder

Heritability: Schizoaffective disorder also shows a strong genetic component, although slightly lower than bipolar disorder. If one identical twin has it, the other has about a 40% chance of developing the condition.

Genetic Overlap: Schizoaffective disorder shares genetic risk factors with both schizophrenia and bipolar disorder. This suggests that some genes influence the development of all three conditions.

Family History: Similar to bipolar disorder, having a family history of schizoaffective disorder, schizophrenia, or bipolar disorder increases your risk.

These disorders are rooted in biology, not personal failings. While genetics play a role, many factors are within our control. Lifestyle changes, therapy, and medication can significantly improve quality of life.

Key Points for Both Disorders:

- **Gene-Environment Interaction:** Genes don't tell the whole story. Environmental factors like stress, trauma, substance abuse, and even infections can interact with genes to trigger or worsen symptoms.

- **Epigenetics:** This field studies how environmental factors can actually change gene expression, affecting how genes function without altering the DNA sequence itself. This adds another layer of complexity to understanding the role of genetics.

- **No Guarantees:** Even with a strong family history, it's important to remember that not everyone will develop these disorders. Genetics increase vulnerability, but they don't determine destiny.

Environmental Factors

While genetics lay the groundwork for vulnerability to bipolar disorder and schizoaffective disorder, environmental factors often act as the trigger, influencing whether, when, and how these conditions manifest. Here's a breakdown of significant environmental contributors:

1. Stressful Life Events:

Trauma: Experiencing significant trauma, such as physical or sexual abuse, neglect, or witnessing violence, can have a profound impact on mental health. Trauma can disrupt brain development and increase vulnerability to both disorders.

Major Life Changes: Even positive changes like moving, starting a new job, or getting married can be stressful. Negative events like the death of a loved one, job loss, or financial difficulties can also significantly increase risk.

2. Substance Abuse:

Drugs and Alcohol: Substance abuse, particularly of drugs like cannabis, cocaine, and amphetamines, can trigger psychotic episodes and worsen the course of both disorders. Alcohol can also disrupt mood and interfere with medication.

3. Social Environment:

Early Childhood Adversity: A lack of stable and nurturing relationships in early childhood can increase vulnerability to mental health problems later in life.

Social Isolation and Loneliness: Lack of social support and connection can exacerbate symptoms and hinder recovery.

4. Physical Health:

Chronic Illness: Having a chronic medical condition can add stress and increase the risk of mental health problems.

Sleep Disturbances: Disrupted sleep patterns are common in both disorders and can worsen symptoms.

Hormonal Changes: Fluctuations in hormones, such as during puberty or menopause, can trigger mood episodes.

5. Other Factors:

Seasonal Changes: Some people experience mood changes with the seasons, particularly in winter (seasonal affective disorder).

Medication Side Effects: Certain medications can sometimes trigger mood or psychotic symptoms.

How these factors contribute:

Triggering Onset: Environmental stressors can trigger the first episode of bipolar disorder or schizoaffective disorder in someone with a genetic predisposition.

Worsening Symptoms: Stress and other factors can exacerbate existing symptoms and increase the frequency and severity of episodes.

Interfering with Treatment: Substance abuse and unhealthy lifestyle choices can hinder the effectiveness of medication and therapy.

These disorders are not caused by personal weakness or character flaws. By managing stress, building healthy relationships, and making positive lifestyle choices, people can reduce their risk and improve their quality of life. Recognizing and addressing environmental triggers can help prevent or delay the onset of symptoms and improve long-term outcomes.

The biopsychosocial model and the interconnectedness of mind and body

Understanding the Biopsychosocial Model

Imagine a three-legged stool. To be stable, it needs all three legs to be strong and balanced. This is the essence of the biopsychosocial model. It tells us that our well-being isn't just about our bodies (biology) but also about our minds (psychology) and our connections to others (social context). These three legs are always interacting, supporting, and sometimes challenging each other.

The Mind-Body Connection in Bipolar and Schizoaffective Disorders

For too long, mental health has been seen as separate from physical health. But the truth is, our minds and bodies are deeply intertwined. What affects one affects the other. This is especially true for conditions like bipolar and schizoaffective disorder.

Think of it this way:

- **The Brain is Part of the Body:** The brain is a physical organ, just like the heart or lungs. It's influenced by physical factors like:
    - **Genetics:** Inherited genes can increase vulnerability.
    - **Brain Chemistry:** Imbalances in neurotransmitters like dopamine and serotonin play a key role.
    - **Stress Response:** How our bodies react to stress can significantly impact mood and thinking.

- **The Body Listens to the Mind:** Our mental and emotional states can have a powerful effect on our physical health.
  - **Stress and the Immune System:** Chronic stress weakens the immune system, making us more susceptible to illness.
  - **The Gut-Brain Connection:** The bacteria in our gut can actually influence our mood and brain function.
  - **Physical Symptoms of Mental Distress:** Conditions like bipolar and schizoaffective disorder often come with physical symptoms like sleep problems, changes in appetite, and fatigue.

Why This Matters for You

Understanding the biopsychosocial model and the mind-body connection empowers you to take a more holistic approach to your well-being. It means:

- **You are not to blame:** These conditions are not a sign of weakness or a character flaw. They result from a complex interplay of factors.

- **You have more control than you think:** While you can't change your genes, you can make choices that support your mental and physical health.

- **Treatment is about more than medication:** While medication can be essential, it's often most effective when combined with therapy, lifestyle changes, and social support.

Taking an Active Role in Your Well-being

Here are some things you can do to support your mental and physical health:

Manage Stress: Find healthy ways to cope with stress, such as mindfulness, exercise, and spending time in nature.

Prioritize Sleep: Aim for 7-9 hours of quality sleep each night.

Nourish Your Body: Eat a balanced diet with plenty of fruits, vegetables, and whole grains.

Connect with Others: Build strong relationships and seek support from loved ones, support groups, or a therapist.

Engage in Mind-Body Practices: Explore techniques like yoga, meditation, and deep breathing to calm your mind and body.

By taking care of yourself—body, mind, and spirit—you can take an active role in your journey toward healing and living a fulfilling life beyond your diagnosis.

Part 2: Finding Your Path to Wellness

Chapter 6

The Importance of Seeking Professional Support

Living with bipolar disorder or schizoaffective disorder can be incredibly challenging, but you don't have to navigate this journey alone. Seeking professional support is crucial for managing these conditions effectively and improving your quality of life. Here's why:

1. Accurate Diagnosis and Personalized Treatment:

- **Differential Diagnosis:** Mental health professionals are trained to distinguish between different conditions with similar symptoms. This is essential because bipolar disorder and schizoaffective disorder can sometimes be mistaken for other conditions like depression, anxiety, or schizophrenia.

- **Individualized Treatment Plans:** A mental health professional will work with you to develop a treatment plan tailored to your specific needs and symptoms. This may involve a combination of medication, therapy, and lifestyle changes.

2. Medication Management:

- **Finding the Right Medication:** Psychiatrists can prescribe medications to help stabilize mood, reduce psychotic symptoms, and improve overall functioning. Finding the right medication and dosage can take time and require careful monitoring by a professional.
- **Managing Side Effects:** Many psychiatric medications have potential side effects. A doctor can help you manage these side effects and make adjustments as needed.
- **Ensuring Medication Safety:** Some medications can interact with each other or with other medical conditions. A doctor can ensure that your medications are safe and effective for you.

3. Therapy for Coping and Growth:

- **Developing Coping Strategies:** Therapists can teach you coping skills to manage symptoms, reduce stress, and improve your overall quality of life.
- **Addressing Underlying Issues:** Therapy can help you explore and address any underlying emotional issues or trauma that may be contributing to your condition.
- **Building a Support System:** Therapy can provide a safe and supportive space to process your experiences and

connect with others who understand what you're going through.

4. Crisis Management and Prevention:

- **Early Intervention:** Mental health professionals can help you identify early warning signs of a mood episode or psychotic episode and intervene to prevent it from escalating.
- **Developing a Crisis Plan:** Working with a therapist, you can create a crisis plan to guide you and your loved ones during difficult times.
- **Access to Emergency Services:** If a crisis occurs, your mental health professional can help you access appropriate emergency services.

5. Long-Term Support and Management:

- **Monitoring Progress:** Regular check-ups with a mental health professional can help monitor your progress and make adjustments to your treatment plan as needed.
- **Maintaining Stability:** Ongoing support can help you stay on track with your treatment and maintain long-term stability.
- **Achieving Your Goals:** A therapist can help you set realistic goals and work towards achieving them, whether

it's improving your relationships, pursuing your passions, or finding fulfilling work.

Treatment Options for Bipolar and Schizoaffective Disorder

Effective treatment for bipolar disorder and schizoaffective disorder often involves a combination of approaches tailored to the individual's specific needs. Here's an overview of common treatment options:

1. **Medications**
- **Mood Stabilizers:** These are often the first line of treatment for bipolar disorder. They help to control mood swings and prevent both manic and depressive episodes.
  - **Lithium:** A classic mood stabilizer that's been used for decades. It's particularly effective in preventing mania.
  - **Anticonvulsants:** Certain medications originally developed to treat seizures have also proven effective in stabilizing mood. Examples include valproic acid (Depakote), lamotrigine (Lamictal), and carbamazepine (Tegretol).

- **Antipsychotics:** These medications can help manage symptoms of psychosis (such as hallucinations or delusions) that sometimes occur during manic episodes. They also have mood-stabilizing properties. Examples include olanzapine (Zyprexa), risperidone (Risperdal), quetiapine (Seroquel), and aripiprazole (Abilify).

- **Antidepressants:** These may be used cautiously to treat depressive episodes in bipolar disorder, often in combination with a mood stabilizer to prevent triggering a manic episode.

2. Therapy

- **Cognitive Behavioral Therapy (CBT):** CBT helps identify and change negative thought patterns and behaviors that contribute to mood episodes and psychotic symptoms. It teaches coping skills for managing stress, improving relationships, and preventing relapse.

- **Interpersonal and Social Rhythm Therapy (IPSRT):** This therapy focuses on stabilizing daily routines, improving interpersonal relationships, and managing stressful life events, which are all crucial for people with bipolar disorder.

- **Family-Focused Therapy (FFT):** FFT helps families understand the illness, improve communication, and develop strategies to support their loved one. This can be particularly helpful for both conditions, as family support is essential.

- **Psychoeducation:** Learning about the illness, its symptoms, and treatment options can empower individuals and their families to manage the condition effectively.

3. Lifestyle Changes

- **Regular Sleep Schedule:** Maintaining a consistent sleep-wake cycle is crucial for mood stability.
- **Healthy Diet:** Eating a balanced diet with plenty of fruits, vegetables, and whole grains can support overall physical and mental health.
- **Regular Exercise:** Physical activity has mood-boosting effects and can help reduce stress.
- **Stress Management Techniques:** Practicing relaxation techniques like mindfulness, meditation, and deep breathing can help manage stress and improve emotional regulation.
- **Avoiding Drugs and Alcohol:** Substance abuse can worsen symptoms and interfere with treatment.

4. Other Treatment Options

- **Electroconvulsive Therapy (ECT):** ECT may be an option for severe cases of bipolar or schizoaffective disorder that haven't responded to other treatments.
- **Transcranial Magnetic Stimulation (TMS):** TMS is a non-invasive procedure that uses magnetic fields to stimulate nerve cells in the brain. It may be helpful for treatment-resistant depression in both conditions.
- **Support Groups:** Connecting with others who have similar experiences can provide valuable support and encouragement.

Finding the Right Treatment

It's important to work with a mental health professional to develop a personalized treatment plan that addresses your specific needs and symptoms. Treatment is often most effective when it combines medication, therapy, and healthy lifestyle choices.

Remember

Recovery is possible: With the right treatment and support, people with bipolar disorder and schizoaffective disorder can live full and meaningful lives.

Treatment is an ongoing process: Managing these conditions is a lifelong journey that requires commitment and self-care.

Don't give up hope: There are many effective treatments available, and with persistence, you can find what works best for you.

Finding the Right Fit: Our Medication Journey

When I first received my bipolar diagnosis, it felt like a huge relief to finally have an explanation for the emotional rollercoaster I'd been riding. But it also meant starting a new chapter in my treatment journey. I was already on medication for anxiety and depression, and now I had to add mood stabilizers to the mix.

The first medication I tried was rough. It made me physically ill, I lost weight, and the side effects were almost unbearable. I felt discouraged, like maybe this was just going to be my new normal. But my psychiatrist encouraged me to keep trying. We switched to a different medication, but that one also brought a host of unpleasant side effects. It took three tries before we finally found the right fit.

I remember the day I realized things were finally shifting. It was subtle at first, like the fog was slowly lifting. My moods felt more stable, the intense highs and lows less frequent. I had more energy, and I could think more clearly. It was incredible.

Of course, medication wasn't a magic cure-all. I continued with therapy, working through the emotional challenges and developing coping mechanisms. But the medication gave me a foundation of stability that allowed me to truly engage in the therapeutic process.

Looking back, I'm grateful for my psychiatrist's patience and persistence. It would have been easy to give up after the first or second medication failed, but he kept reminding me that finding the right treatment is often a process of trial and error. And he was right.

My experience taught me the importance of:

- **Advocating for myself:** Speaking up about how I was feeling, both good and bad.
- **Being patient:** Understanding that finding the right medication can take time.
- **Working closely with my doctor:** Communicating openly and honestly about my symptoms and side effects.

My own struggles with finding the right medication were mirrored in my son's experience, although his experiences were before mine. Seeing him go through the trial-and-error process was stressful, but it also strengthened our bond and deepened my understanding of the challenges of schizoaffective disorder.

It was tough to watch him struggle, but we persevered. We worked closely with his doctor, kept detailed records of his symptoms and side effects, and never gave up hope. Finally, after several adjustments, we found a medication combination that made a world of difference.

Witnessing his transformation was incredible. It reinforced the message that finding the right treatment is possible, even when the journey is long and difficult. It also highlighted the importance of:

- **Parental support:** Being there for my son, offering encouragement, and advocating for his needs.
- **Open communication:** Talking openly and honestly with him about his experiences and concerns.
- **Collaboration with his healthcare team:** Working together to find the best treatment plan for him.

Our shared journey has taught me that while bipolar disorder and schizoaffective disorder presents unique challenges for every individual, the power of perseverance, hope, and family support can make all the difference.

If you're struggling to find the right medication, please don't give up hope. It's out there. Keep working with your doctor, keep advocating for yourself, and trust that you will find the treatment that helps you feel your best.

Don't hesitate to reach out.

If you're struggling with symptoms of bipolar disorder or schizoaffective disorder, please reach out to a mental health professional. It's a sign of strength, not weakness, to ask for help. With the right support, you can live a full and meaningful life beyond your diagnosis.

Chapter 7

Coping Mechanisms and Self-Care

Managing bipolar disorder or schizoaffective disorder is a marathon, not a sprint. It requires consistent effort and a commitment to building a foundation of well-being. Self-care, stress management, and healthy habits are not just "nice-to-haves" but essential tools for navigating the challenges of these conditions and living a fulfilling life.

Why are they so important?

Bipolar and schizoaffective disorders are characterized by significant mood fluctuations. Self-care practices, stress reduction techniques, and healthy habits help stabilize mood, reducing the intensity and frequency of episodes.

Stress is a major trigger for both conditions. By actively managing stress, you can reduce its impact on your mental and physical health.

Self-care and healthy habits build resilience, giving you the strength and resources to cope with challenges and setbacks.

When you prioritize your well-being, you create a life that is more balanced, enjoyable, and fulfilling.

1. Lifestyle Management

- **Routine, Routine, Routine:** Establish a consistent daily routine for sleep, meals, and activities. This helps regulate your body's natural rhythms and can improve mood stability.

- **Prioritize Sleep:** Aim for 7-9 hours of quality sleep each night. Disrupted sleep can trigger mood episodes and worsen symptoms.

- **Healthy Diet:** Nourish your body with a balanced diet rich in fruits, vegetables, and whole grains. Avoid excessive sugar, caffeine, and alcohol, which can disrupt mood and sleep.

- **Regular Exercise:** Physical activity has mood-boosting effects and can help reduce stress. Find activities you enjoy and make them a regular part of your routine.

2. Stress Management

- **Mindfulness and Meditation:** These practices can help you become more aware of your thoughts and feelings without judgment, reducing stress and promoting emotional regulation.

- **Relaxation Techniques:** Explore techniques like deep breathing exercises, progressive muscle relaxation, and guided imagery to calm your mind and body.

- **Yoga and Tai Chi:** These practices combine physical postures, breathing exercises, and meditation to promote relaxation, reduce stress, and improve overall well-being.

- **Spending Time in Nature:** Connecting with nature has been shown to reduce stress and improve mood.

3. Social Support and Connection

- **Strong Relationships:** Nurture healthy relationships with family and friends who offer support and understanding.

- **Support Groups:** Connect with others who have similar experiences in support groups or online communities. Sharing your experiences and learning from others can be incredibly validating and empowering.

- **Therapy:** Therapy provides a safe and supportive space to explore your challenges, develop coping skills, and improve your relationships.

4. Self-Monitoring and Early Intervention

- **Mood Tracking:** Keep a mood journal to track your mood patterns, identify triggers, and recognize early warning signs of mood episodes.

- **Symptom Management:** Develop a plan for managing specific symptoms, such as strategies for dealing with anxiety, racing thoughts, or low motivation.

- **Early Intervention:** If you notice early warning signs of a mood episode, take action immediately. This might involve reaching out to your therapist, adjusting your medication, or practicing relaxation techniques.

5. Cognitive Strategies

- **Challenge Negative Thoughts:** Learn to identify and challenge negative or distorted thinking patterns that contribute to depression or anxiety.

- **Develop Positive Self-Talk:** Practice replacing negative self-talk with positive and encouraging statements.

- **Focus on Your Strengths:** Recognize and appreciate your strengths and accomplishments.

6. Creative Outlets and Hobbies

- **Engage in Activities You Enjoy:** Make time for hobbies and activities that bring you joy and relaxation. This could include painting, writing, music, gardening, or spending time with pets.
- **Express Yourself Creatively:** Creative outlets can be a healthy way to process emotions and experiences.

7. Self-Care

- **Prioritize Self-Care:** Make time for activities that nourish your mind, body, and spirit. This might include taking a relaxing bath, reading a good book, spending time in nature, or getting a massage.
- **Set Boundaries:** Learn to say no to things that drain your energy or trigger stress. Protect your time and energy for activities that support your well-being.
- **Practice Self-Compassion:** Be kind to yourself, especially during difficult times. Remember that setbacks are a normal part of the journey.

Experiment with different coping strategies to discover what helps you manage your symptoms and improve your well-being. Recovery is a journey, not a destination. There will be ups and downs along the way. Don't hesitate to reach out to a mental health professional for guidance and support. By developing a toolbox of coping strategies, you can take an active role in managing your condition and live a fulfilling life beyond your diagnosis.

Creating a foundation of well-being is an ongoing process. It requires commitment, patience, and self-compassion. Start by making small changes and gradually build on your successes.

Finding My Rhythm: Nature, Movement, and Self-Awareness

My journey towards stability has been paved with discoveries, not just of medications and therapies, but also of personal coping strategies that truly resonate with me. One of the most powerful tools in my arsenal has been the combination of movement and nature.

It started with walking. My therapist suggested I spend more time outdoors, and I began with simple walks around my neighborhood. Gradually, I found myself drawn to longer walks, exploring parks and trails, noticing the subtle shifts in the seasons. There's a peacefulness in nature that calms my mind and soothes my soul.

Over time, those walks evolved into runs. Now, I run 5-6 miles most days, but I still make a point of pausing to appreciate the beauty around me – the sunlight filtering through leaves, the fresh cool air and the sound of birds, the feel of the earth beneath my feet-. It's a moving meditation that helps me center myself and connect with something larger than myself.

Gardening has become another source of solace. There's something deeply satisfying about nurturing plants, watching them grow and thrive. When the weather permits, I lose myself in the rhythm of digging, planting, and tending to my garden. It's a grounding experience that helps me feel connected to the earth and the natural cycles of life.

But coping isn't just about external activities. It's also about developing a deep understanding of myself. After my diagnosis, I started paying closer attention to my inner landscape – my thoughts, feelings, and physical sensations. I've learned to recognize the subtle signs that a mood episode might be approaching, allowing me to take proactive steps to manage it.

This self-awareness has also allowed me to communicate more effectively with my loved ones. I've explained what happens during an episode, the signs to watch for, and how they can best support me. This shared understanding has strengthened our relationships and created a safety net during challenging times.

My journey has taught me that coping with bipolar disorder is an ongoing process of self-discovery and adaptation. It's about finding the rhythms and practices that bring balance and stability to my life. It's about connecting with nature, moving my body, and tuning into my inner world. And it's about sharing my experiences with others, creating a network of support and understanding.

Chapter 8

Navigating Relationships and Support Systems

The Ripple Effect: How Bipolar and Schizoaffective Disorders Impact Family Dynamics and Relationships

A diagnosis of bipolar disorder or schizoaffective disorder doesn't just affect the individual; it sends ripples throughout the entire family system. These conditions can bring significant challenges to family dynamics and relationships, but they can also foster resilience, understanding, and deeper connections.

Challenges

Emotional Rollercoaster: The unpredictable mood swings and symptoms can be difficult for family members to understand and cope with. This can lead to feelings of frustration, worry, fear, and even resentment.

Communication Difficulties: During mood episodes, communication can become strained. Mania may involve rapid speech, racing thoughts, and irritability, while depression can lead to withdrawal and isolation.

Changes in Roles and Responsibilities: Family members may need to take on additional responsibilities, such as managing finances, providing care, or making decisions for their loved one. This can disrupt family roles and create tension.

Financial Strain: The cost of treatment, lost income due to disability, and impulsive spending during manic episodes can put a strain on family finances.

Social Isolation: Families may withdraw from social activities due to the stigma associated with mental illness or the challenges of managing their loved one's symptoms in public.

Strain on Relationships: The stress of managing the illness can put a strain on relationships, particularly between spouses or partners.

Positive Impacts

Increased Empathy and Understanding: Navigating these challenges can lead to increased empathy and understanding within the family. Family members may learn to appreciate the strength and resilience of their loved one and develop a deeper understanding of mental health.

Stronger Bonds: Shared experiences and mutual support can strengthen family bonds. Families may come together to provide care, advocate for their loved one, and celebrate their successes.

Improved Communication: Learning to communicate effectively about the illness and its challenges can improve family communication overall.

Increased Resilience: Facing adversity together can build resilience within the family, equipping them to handle future challenges with greater strength and understanding.

Tips for Navigating Family Dynamics

Open Communication: Encourage open and honest communication about the illness, its challenges, and everyone's needs.

Education: Learn as much as you can about bipolar disorder or schizoaffective disorder. This will help you understand your loved one's experiences and provide better support.

Family Therapy: Family therapy can provide a safe space to address challenges, improve communication, and develop coping strategies.

Support Groups: Connect with other families who are facing similar challenges. Sharing experiences and learning from others can be incredibly helpful.

Self-Care: Remember to prioritize your own well-being. Take breaks, engage in activities you enjoy, and seek support when you need it.

The Power of Support: A Lifeline in Managing Bipolar and Schizoaffective Disorders

Living with bipolar disorder or schizoaffective disorder can be an isolating experience, but it doesn't have to be. Support from others is absolutely crucial for navigating the challenges, maintaining stability, and living a fulfilling life. It's not just a "nice-to-have," but an essential element of the recovery journey.

Why is support so critical?

Reduces Isolation: These conditions can lead to feelings of isolation and loneliness. Connecting with others who understand creates a sense of belonging and shared experience, reminding you that you're not alone.

Provides Emotional Validation: Having someone listen without judgment and validate your experiences can be incredibly healing. It helps you feel seen, heard, and understood.

Offers Practical Assistance: Support can come in many forms, including practical help with daily tasks, transportation, childcare, or financial assistance. This can alleviate stress and free up energy for self-care and recovery.

Encourages Treatment Adherence: Loved ones can encourage you to stick to your treatment plan, even when it's difficult. They can provide reminders, offer encouragement, and help you navigate challenges.

Promotes Early Intervention: Supportive individuals can often recognize early warning signs of mood episodes and help you take proactive steps to prevent escalation.

Fosters Hope and Resilience: Knowing that you have people you can count on can provide a sense of hope and resilience during difficult times. It reminds you that you have the strength to persevere.

Where to Find Support

Family and Friends: Loved ones can offer emotional support, practical assistance, and encouragement. Open communication and education about the illness are key to building strong support networks.

Support Groups: Connecting with others who have similar experiences can be incredibly validating and empowering. Support groups provide a safe space to share your story, learn from others, and build community.

Mental Health Professionals: Therapists, psychiatrists, and other mental health professionals offer specialized support, guidance, and treatment. They can help you develop coping strategies, manage symptoms, and navigate challenges.

Online Communities: Online forums and communities can provide a sense of connection and support, especially for those who may not have access to in-person support groups.

Building a Support System

Communicate Your Needs: Don't be afraid to ask for help when you need it. Let your loved ones know what kind of support would be most helpful.

Educate Others: Help your family and friends understand your condition and how they can best support you.

Set Boundaries: It's okay to set boundaries to protect your energy and well-being. Let people know what you're comfortable sharing and what your limits are.

Be Open to Receiving: Allow yourself to receive support, even if it feels uncomfortable at first. Remember that accepting help is a sign of strength, not weakness.

The Unveiling: How Bipolar Showed Me True Support (and Where It Was Lacking)

Receiving my bipolar diagnosis was a complex moment. There was relief in finally understanding the turbulent emotions I'd battled for so long, but also a wave of fear and sadness. I was already struggling with anxiety and depression, facing personal challenges, and now this. How would I cope with it all?

Thankfully, I wasn't alone. My true friends and my family stepped up. They checked in regularly, offering a listening ear and a shoulder to lean on. Their presence was a lifeline during those dark days when the extra stress exacerbated my symptoms, despite medication. My therapist, too, was incredibly understanding, providing consistent support and guidance.

Even my son, navigating his own challenges with schizoaffective disorder, showed empathy and understanding. He knew what it meant to struggle with mental health, and his support was a source of strength.

But the diagnosis also acted as a filter, revealing the true nature of my relationships. Some "friends" vanished after I shared my diagnosis, unable or unwilling to handle the reality of mental illness. It was painful, but it also clarified who truly mattered.

The diagnosis also shed light on some of my personal relationships, providing answers to long-held questions about their dynamics. It was a difficult realization, but it ultimately paved the way for healthier connections.

Now, I cherish the people who remain. I'm fortunate to have someone who not only cares deeply but is actively learning about bipolar disorder and the nuances of my moods. It's an ongoing process, but their willingness to understand means the world.

While I still feel a twinge of self-consciousness at times, I've come to realize that bipolar disorder doesn't define me. It's a part of me, but it doesn't diminish my worth or my ability to live a full life.

By getting in tune with my emotions and recognizing the early signs of an episode, I've gained a sense of control. I've developed coping skills and strategies to navigate the challenges, and with each passing day, I grow more confident in my ability to manage this condition.

More than anything, this journey has taught me the immeasurable value of genuine support. It's a reminder that even in the darkest moments, we don't have to struggle alone.

Chapter 9

Thriving in Everyday Life

Navigating Daily Life: Practical Strategies for Living with Bipolar and Schizoaffective Disorders

While managing your mental health is a priority, life doesn't stop. Work, school, finances, and daily routines can all be impacted by bipolar and schizoaffective disorders. But with proactive strategies and the right support, you can navigate these practical aspects of life with greater ease and confidence.

1. Work and School

- **Disclosure:** Deciding whether to disclose your diagnosis is a personal choice. Consider the potential benefits (support, accommodations) and drawbacks (stigma, discrimination) in your specific situation.
- **Accommodations:** If you choose to disclose, explore accommodations that can help you succeed, such as flexible work hours, quiet workspaces, or extended deadlines for assignments.
- **Stress Management:** Work and school can be stressful environments. Develop coping mechanisms to manage

stress, such as taking breaks, practicing mindfulness, or utilizing support resources.

- **Open Communication:** Maintain open communication with your employer, teachers, or supervisors about your needs and any challenges you may be facing.

2. Finances

- **Budgeting and Planning:** Create a budget to track your income and expenses. This can help you identify potential financial stressors and develop strategies to manage them.

- **Financial Assistance:** Explore resources that may be available to you, such as disability benefits, government assistance programs, or financial counseling.

- **Impulsive Spending:** If you experience impulsive spending during manic episodes, consider strategies to limit access to funds or enlist the help of a trusted friend or family member to manage finances.

3. Daily Routines

- **Consistency is Key:** Establish a consistent daily routine for sleep, meals, medication, and activities. This helps regulate your body's natural rhythms and can improve mood stability.

- **Prioritize Sleep:** Aim for 7-9 hours of quality sleep each night. Create a relaxing bedtime routine and avoid stimulating activities before bed.

- **Healthy Lifestyle:** Nourish your body with a balanced diet, engage in regular exercise, and limit substance use. These healthy habits support both physical and mental well-being.

- **Planning and Organization:** Use tools like calendars, to-do lists, and reminders to stay organized and manage your time effectively.

4. Relationships

- **Open Communication:** Communicate openly and honestly with your loved ones about your condition and your needs.

- **Education:** Help your family and friends understand your condition and how they can best support you.

- **Boundaries:** Set healthy boundaries to protect your energy and well-being.

- **Quality Time:** Make time for meaningful connections with loved ones.

5. Self-Advocacy

- **Know Your Rights:** Understand your rights regarding employment, education, and healthcare.
- **Seek Support:** Don't hesitate to reach out to mental health professionals, support groups, or advocacy organizations for assistance and guidance.
- **Empower Yourself:** Take an active role in your treatment and self-care.

Remember:

Small Changes Make a Difference: Start by making small, manageable changes to your routine and gradually build on your successes.

Be Patient with Yourself: Progress may not always be linear. There will be challenges and setbacks along the way.

Celebrate Your Successes: Acknowledge and celebrate your achievements, no matter how small they may seem.

By addressing these practical aspects of life, you can create a more stable and supportive environment for yourself, empowering you to live a full and meaningful life despite the challenges of bipolar or schizoaffective disorder.

Tips for Managing Challenges and Maintaining Stability with Bipolar and Schizoaffective Disorders

Living with bipolar or schizoaffective disorder requires ongoing effort to manage challenges and maintain stability. But by developing a proactive and personalized approach, you can navigate the ups and downs with greater resilience and confidence. Here are some tips to help you on your journey:

1. Know Yourself

- **Identify Your Triggers:** Pay close attention to your mood patterns and identify the situations, people, or events that tend to trigger mood episodes.
- **Recognize Early Warning Signs:** Learn to recognize the subtle signs that a mood episode may be approaching. This allows you to take proactive steps to manage it.
- **Understand Your Strengths and Weaknesses:** Acknowledge your strengths and build on them. Be aware of your vulnerabilities and develop strategies to manage them.

2. Prioritize Self-Care

- **Make it a Daily Practice:** Self-care isn't a luxury; it's a necessity. Incorporate self-care activities into your daily routine, even if it's just for a few minutes.

- **Find What Nourishes You:** Explore different activities and find what truly helps you recharge and feel your best. This might include spending time in nature, pursuing hobbies, practicing relaxation techniques, or connecting with loved ones.

- **Be Kind to Yourself:** Treat yourself with compassion and understanding, especially during difficult times. Remember that setbacks are a normal part of the journey.

3. Build a Strong Support System

- **Connect with Others:** Reach out to family, friends, support groups, or mental health professionals for support and encouragement.

- **Communicate Openly:** Share your experiences and needs with your loved ones. Help them understand your condition and how they can best support you.

- **Set Boundaries:** Don't be afraid to set boundaries to protect your energy and well-being.

4. Manage Stress Effectively

- **Identify Stressors:** Become aware of the sources of stress in your life.

- **Develop Coping Mechanisms:** Build a toolbox of healthy coping strategies, such as mindfulness, exercise, deep breathing, or spending time in nature.

- **Seek Professional Help:** If stress feels overwhelming, don't hesitate to seek professional guidance from a therapist or counselor.

5. Maintain a Healthy Lifestyle

- **Prioritize Sleep:** Establish a consistent sleep schedule and create a relaxing bedtime routine.
- **Nourishing Diet:** Fuel your body with a balanced diet rich in fruits, vegetables, and whole grains. Limit processed foods, sugary drinks, and excessive caffeine.
- **Regular Exercise:** Find physical activities you enjoy and make them a regular part of your routine.
- **Limit Substance Use:** Avoid alcohol and drugs, which can worsen symptoms and interfere with treatment.

6. Stay Organized and Plan Ahead

- **Create a Routine:** Establish a consistent daily routine to provide structure and stability.
- **Use Planning Tools:** Utilize calendars, to-do lists, and reminders to stay organized and manage your time effectively.
- **Break Down Tasks:** If large tasks feel overwhelming, break them down into smaller, more manageable steps.

7. Be Patient and Persistent

- **Focus on Progress, Not Perfection:** Recovery is a journey, not a destination. There will be ups and downs along the way.
- **Celebrate Your Successes:** Acknowledge and celebrate your achievements, no matter how small they may seem.
- **Don't Give Up:** Remember that you are not alone. With persistence and the right support, you can live a fulfilling life beyond your diagnosis.

By implementing these tips and developing a personalized approach to managing your condition, you can navigate challenges with greater resilience, maintain stability, and create a life filled with meaning and purpose.

Part 3: Embracing Hope and Finding Meaning

Chapter 10

Living a Life of Purpose

It's easy to feel defined by a diagnosis of bipolar disorder or schizoaffective disorder. The labels can feel heavy, the symptoms overwhelming. But it's crucial to remember that you are so much more than your diagnosis. You are a unique individual with your own strengths, passions, and aspirations. Finding meaning and purpose beyond the diagnosis is not just possible, it's essential for living a fulfilling life.

Why is it important?

Provides Direction and Motivation: Having a sense of purpose gives you something to strive for, even when faced with challenges. It provides a sense of direction and motivation, helping you stay focused on your goals and values.

Enhances Resilience: When you have a sense of meaning in your life, you're better equipped to handle setbacks and challenges. It gives you a reason to keep going, even when things get tough.

Reduces Stigma: Focusing on your passions and purpose helps shift the focus away from the illness and reduces the stigma associated with mental health conditions.

Promotes Self-Worth: Engaging in activities that bring you joy and fulfillment boosts your self-esteem and sense of self-worth.

Increases Overall Well-being: Studies have shown that having a sense of purpose is linked to greater happiness, life satisfaction, and overall well-being.

How to Find Meaning and Purpose

Explore Your Values: What is truly important to you? What are your core values and beliefs? Identifying your values can help you make choices that align with your sense of purpose.

Connect with Your Passions: What activities bring you joy and fulfillment? What are you passionate about? Engaging in your passions can provide a sense of meaning and purpose.

Set Meaningful Goals: Set goals that are aligned with your values and passions. These could be personal goals, career goals, or goals related to helping others.

Contribute to Something Larger Than Yourself: Find ways to contribute to your community or to a cause you care about. Volunteering, activism, or creative expression can all provide a sense of purpose.

Cultivate Gratitude: Focus on the positive aspects of your life and express gratitude for the people and things you cherish. Gratitude can foster a sense of meaning and appreciation.

Mindfulness and Self-Reflection: Engage in mindfulness practices or self-reflection to connect with your inner self and explore what truly matters to you.

Finding meaning and purpose is an ongoing process of self-discovery and exploration. It may take time to discover what truly gives your life meaning. Don't be afraid to experiment and try new things. Your journey to meaning and purpose will be unique to you. Embrace your individuality and follow your own path.

Pursuing Passions and Connecting with Values

Living with bipolar or schizoaffective disorder can bring challenges, but it doesn't have to define your life. In fact, it can be a catalyst for self-discovery and a deeper understanding of what truly matters. By pursuing your passions and connecting with your values, you can unlock a sense of purpose and fulfillment that transcends the limitations of your diagnosis.

The Power of Passions

Passions are the fire that ignites our soul. They are the activities, interests, and pursuits that bring us joy, energy, and a sense of aliveness. When we engage in our passions, we tap into a source of creativity, motivation, and resilience that can help us navigate the challenges of life.

- **Discovering Your Passions:**

    - Reflect on activities that bring you joy, excitement, or a sense of flow.
    - Explore new hobbies and interests.
    - Recall what you loved doing as a child.
    - Pay attention to what sparks your curiosity.

- **Nurturing Your Passions:**

  - Make time for your passions, even if it's just for a few minutes each day.
  - Don't be afraid to try new things and step outside your comfort zone.
  - Surround yourself with people who support your passions.
  - Celebrate your achievements and progress.

The Importance of Values

Values are the guiding principles that shape our lives. They are the beliefs and ideals that we hold dear, such as honesty, compassion, creativity, or justice. When we live in alignment with our values, we create a life that is meaningful and authentic.

- **Identifying Your Values:**

  - Consider what is truly important to you.
  - Reflect on the qualities you admire in others.
  - Think about the causes you care about.
  - Pay attention to what makes you feel proud or fulfilled.

- **Living Your Values:**

  - Make choices that align with your values.
  - Speak up for what you believe in.
  - Surround yourself with people who share your values.
  - Use your values to guide your actions and decisions.

The Intersection of Passions and Values

When we pursue our passions in a way that aligns with our values, we create a powerful synergy that can transform our lives. This synergy can lead to a deeper sense of purpose, increased self-worth, and greater resilience in the face of challenges.

Redefining "Normal": Embracing the Spectrum of Human Experience

Society often tries to squeeze us into neat little boxes, labeling anything outside the lines as "abnormal." But who gets to define what's normal, anyway? Living with bipolar or schizoaffective disorder challenges those narrow definitions and invites us to embrace a broader, more inclusive understanding of what it means to be human.

Challenging Expectations

The Myth of "Perfect" Mental Health: Society often paints a picture of mental health as a state of constant happiness and stability. But this is an unrealistic and unattainable ideal. We all experience a range of emotions, challenges, and setbacks. It's time to acknowledge that mental health is a journey, not a destination.

Embracing Neurodiversity: Our brains are as unique as our fingerprints. Bipolar and schizoaffective disorders are part of the spectrum of human neurodiversity. Instead of viewing these conditions as "abnormal," we can appreciate them as variations that bring unique perspectives and strengths to the world.

Reframing "Symptoms" as Experiences: The experiences associated with these conditions, such as intense emotions, heightened creativity, or altered perceptions, can be challenging, but they can also be sources of insight, growth, and connection.

Questioning Societal Norms: Many societal norms are based on outdated assumptions about mental health. It's time to challenge these norms and create a more inclusive and accepting society for all.

Redefining "Normal"

Uniqueness, Not Uniformity: "Normal" is not a one-size-fits-all concept. It's about embracing our individuality and recognizing that there is no single "right" way to be.

Strength in Vulnerability: Living with these conditions often requires immense strength, resilience, and self-awareness. These qualities should be recognized and celebrated, not stigmatized.

Growth Through Challenges: The challenges of living with bipolar or schizoaffective disorder can lead to profound personal growth, self-discovery, and a deeper understanding of oneself and the world.

Connection and Community: By sharing our experiences and supporting each other, we can create a sense of community and belonging that transcends the limitations of societal expectations.

Embracing Your Unique Tapestry: Strengths and Experiences

Living with bipolar or schizoaffective disorder is undeniably a challenge. It's a journey filled with highs and lows, unexpected turns, and moments of intense struggle. But within those experiences, within the very fabric of who you are, lies a unique tapestry of strengths and insights waiting to be embraced.

Your Experiences, Your Teachers

It's tempting to view your experiences through a lens of negativity, focusing on the challenges and limitations. But what if you shifted your perspective? What if you saw your experiences as teachers, offering valuable lessons and shaping you into the resilient individual you are today?

Resilience Forged in Fire: Navigating the turbulent waters of mood episodes builds resilience like nothing else. You've learned to weather storms, adapt to change, and rise again, stronger than before.

Empathy Born from Understanding: Living with these conditions fosters a deep understanding of human emotion and struggle. You possess a unique capacity for empathy and compassion, allowing you to connect with others on a profound level.

Creativity Sparked by Intensity: Many individuals with bipolar or schizoaffective disorder experience heightened creativity and a unique perspective on the world. Embrace this creative spark and allow it to fuel your self-expression.

Self-Awareness as a Superpower: The journey of managing these conditions often leads to profound self-awareness. You've learned to recognize your triggers, understand your patterns, and tune in to your inner world.

Your Strengths, Your Guiding Stars

Beyond the challenges, you possess a unique set of strengths that can guide you towards a fulfilling life. These strengths may have been honed through your experiences, or they may be innate qualities that shine through.

Perseverance: You've learned to persevere through difficult times, never giving up on your journey towards stability and well-being.

Courage: It takes courage to face the challenges of these conditions head-on and to live authentically in a world that doesn't always understand.

Compassion: You possess a deep capacity for empathy and compassion, both for yourself and for others who are struggling.

Creativity: Your unique perspective and experiences can fuel your creativity in a multitude of ways.

Embracing Your Whole Self

Embrace your experiences, both the challenging and the empowering. Embrace your strengths, the ones that have carried you through and the ones that are waiting to be discovered. You are a complex, multifaceted individual with a unique story to tell.

Chapter 11

A Message of Hope

This journey with bipolar or schizoaffective disorder may be challenging, but it is also a journey of resilience, self-discovery, and profound growth. You are not alone. Thousands of others are navigating similar paths, facing similar struggles, and discovering their own unique strengths along the way.

Remember these key truths:

You are not your diagnosis. You are a complex, multifaceted individual with your own passions, talents, and dreams. Don't let the diagnosis define you.

Recovery is possible. It may not be a linear path, but with the right support, treatment, and self-care, you can live a full and meaningful life.

Your experiences have value. Even the most challenging experiences can teach you valuable lessons, build resilience, and foster empathy.

You are stronger than you think. You have already overcome so much. Trust in your inner strength and your ability to navigate whatever comes your way.

There is hope. Never give up hope. There is always light at the end of the tunnel, even when it's hard to see.

Embrace the Journey

This journey may be unpredictable, but it is also an opportunity for growth, self-discovery, and connection. Embrace the ups and downs, the challenges and triumphs. Learn from your experiences, celebrate your strengths, and find joy in the everyday moments.

Reach Out for Support

You don't have to go through this alone. Reach out to your loved ones, connect with others who understand, and seek professional support when you need it. There is a community of people who care and want to help you succeed.

Live with Purpose

Beyond the diagnosis, there is a life waiting to be lived. Pursue your passions, connect with your values, and find meaning in your experiences. Make a difference in the world, even if it's just in your own small way.

Believe in Yourself

Believe in your ability to heal, to grow, and to live a fulfilling life. You are capable of more than you know. Embrace your journey, trust in your strength, and never give up on your dreams.

You are not alone. You are strong. You are worthy. And you are capable of amazing things.

CONCLUSION

As you reach the end of this journey through the pages of "Beyond the Diagnosis," I hope you carry with you these key takeaways:

Understanding the Conditions

Bipolar and schizoaffective disorders are complex but manageable. They are rooted in biological factors, but environmental influences and personal choices play a significant role in how they manifest.

The biopsychosocial model is essential. It emphasizes the interconnectedness of mind, body, and social context in understanding and managing these conditions.

Genetics and family history increase risk, but don't dictate destiny. While genetics play a role, environmental factors and lifestyle choices can significantly influence the course of these illnesses.

The Power of Support

You are not alone. Thousands of others share similar experiences. Connect with them, build a support system, and lean on those who care.

Support comes in many forms. From family and friends to therapists and support groups, there are various sources of strength and encouragement available.

Open communication is key. Share your experiences, educate your loved ones, and advocate for your needs.

Embracing Your Journey:

Recovery is possible. It's not always linear, but with persistence, self-care, and the right treatment, you can live a full and meaningful life.

Your experiences have value. Even the most challenging times can lead to growth, resilience, and a deeper understanding of yourself.

Embrace your strengths. You possess unique strengths and abilities. Recognize them, cultivate them, and let them guide you.

Finding Meaning and Purpose

You are more than your diagnosis. Don't let it define you. Pursue your passions, connect with your values, and find purpose beyond the illness.

Challenge societal expectations. Redefine "normal" and embrace the diverse spectrum of human experience.

Believe in yourself. You are capable of amazing things. Never give up on your dreams.

Final Words of Hope

This journey may be challenging, but it is also an opportunity for growth, self-discovery, and connection. Embrace your unique path, trust in your resilience, and never lose hope. You are not alone. You are strong. You are worthy. And you are capable of living a fulfilling life beyond the diagnosis.

My New Normal

Finding Rhythm in the Ups and Downs

Life with bipolar disorder is a dance – a constant ebb and flow between moods, energy levels, and perspectives. It's not easy. Some days, the weight of it all feels heavy, the anxiety and depression a constant hum beneath the surface. And then there's my son, navigating his own journey with schizoaffective disorder, adding another layer of complexity to our lives.

There are moments when giving up seems like the easiest option. But then something inside me – call it faith, call it stubbornness, call it the will to live – pulls me back from the brink.

My diagnosis forced a change of pace. I'm no longer working, but I refuse to let it define me. I fill my days with purpose, exploring new interests, volunteering, and simply learning to be present with myself. This time has allowed me to get intimately acquainted with my inner landscape, to understand the nuances of my moods and recognize the subtle shifts that signal an approaching episode.

Sometimes, when I observe the behavior of people who claim to have bipolar disorder, I question whether my own behavior has ever been as erratic or dramatic. It's frustrating to witness individuals use bipolar as an excuse for their actions, especially when they haven't received an actual diagnosis. This trivialization further stigmatizes those of us who genuinely struggle with the condition.

Every day is different. Some days are bright and full of energy, while others are shrouded in a gray mist of depression. I've learned to adapt, to embrace this "new normal" and find a rhythm within the fluctuations. On the days when I feel an episode looming, I prioritize self-care. I relax, breathe deeply, and remind myself that this too shall pass.

My friends have become incredibly attuned to my emotional state. They can hear it in my voice, sense it in my words. Their support is invaluable, a constant reminder that I'm not alone in this dance.

Therapy continues to be a cornerstone of my well-being. That weekly hour provides a safe space to process my experiences, explore my emotions, and develop coping strategies. It's a lifeline, a constant source of support and guidance.

Living with bipolar disorder is an ongoing journey of self-discovery and adaptation. It's about finding a rhythm within the chaos, learning to ride the waves, and embracing the full spectrum of my experience. It's about accepting the challenges, celebrating the triumphs, and never losing sight of hope."

Epilogue

The Unfolding Path

Five years have passed since that initial wave of fear and uncertainty crashed over me with my son's diagnosis and over a year for mine. The world seemed to tilt, the ground unsteady beneath my feet. But as the dust settled, I found myself not broken, but changed. The landscape of my life has shifted, rearranged by the forces of bipolar disorder, and amidst the changes, something unexpected has blossomed: a sense of peace, a hard-won resilience.

It's not that the challenges have vanished. The anxiety still whispers, a subtle tremor in my chest some mornings, a constant companion to the bipolar's unpredictable moods. The depression still casts its shadow at times, a grayness that seeps in around the edges of my vision, a persistent undercurrent to the emotional tides. And my son's journey with schizoaffective disorder continues, a parallel path with its own unique set of triumphs and struggles. But we've learned. We've adapted. We've found a way to navigate these currents with greater awareness and resilience.

My days have found a rhythm, a gentle cadence that honors both the highs and the lows. The mornings begin with mindfulness, a quiet moment on the porch with a cup of coffee, the rising sun painting the sky with hues of hope. It's a time to ground myself, to connect with my breath, to set an intention for the day ahead.

Running remains my sanctuary, a refuge from the noise of the world. Five miles, sometimes more – the pavement a steady drumbeat beneath my feet, worries fading with each stride. And yet, I've learned to pause, to truly see the world around me. The sunlight filtering through leaves, the vibrant hues of a wildflower blooming by the roadside, the symphony of birdsong in the early morning air – these moments of beauty anchor me to the present, a reminder of the simple joys that life offers.

The garden, once a neglected patch of earth, now thrives. Rows of vibrant vegetables, fragrant herbs, and colorful blooms paint a tapestry of life. It's a testament to the nurturing I've poured into it, mirroring the care I now give myself. Each seed planted, each weed pulled, each blossom nurtured – a tangible reminder of growth, resilience, and the power of tending to both the soil and the soul. Evenings are often spent in quiet reflection; a good book, movie or tv show transports me to other realms, offering solace and escape.

Work has taken on a new form, a deeper meaning.   It's a privilege to transform my challenges into a source of strength for others, to offer hope and companionship on a journey that can often feel isolating.

My friendships have deepened, the bonds forged in the fires of shared experience. The ones who weathered the storm of my diagnosis remain my steadfast anchors, their understanding a constant source of comfort. And new connections have blossomed, born from the shared language of vulnerability and resilience.

My relationship with my son has blossomed into a profound source of mutual support. We are fellow travelers on this winding path, each with our own unique map. We understand each other's struggles, the subtle shifts in mood, the weight of invisible burdens. We celebrate each other's victories, the small triumphs of daily life, the moments of clarity and connection. And we navigate the complexities of our conditions together, a testament to the enduring power of family and the bond of love.

Life with bipolar disorder is still a dance, but the steps are more familiar now. I've learned to recognize the music, anticipate the rhythm, and find my own flow within the movement. It's a dance of self-discovery, resilience, and hope. A dance that embraces the full spectrum of my being, the light and the shadow, the joy and the sorrow, the quiet moments of peace and the exhilarating bursts of energy.

The path ahead remains unknown, a winding road with twists and turns yet to be revealed. But I face it with a sense of grounded optimism, a quiet confidence born from years of navigating the unpredictable terrain of my own mind. There will be challenges, undoubtedly. But there will also be moments of joy, connection, and profound meaning. And through it all, I will continue to embrace the unfolding path, knowing that within the tapestry of my experience, there is strength, beauty, and an will to live a life filled with purpose and love.

Resources for Further Support

Organizations

National Alliance on Mental Illness (NAMI): NAMI provides support, education, advocacy, and public awareness programs for people with mental health conditions and their families.

Website: nami.org   HelpLine: 1-800-950-NAMI (6264)

Depression and Bipolar Support Alliance (DBSA): DBSA offers support groups, educational resources, and online tools for people living with mood disorders.   Website: dbsalliance.org

MentalHealth.gov: This government website provides information on various mental health conditions, treatment options, and resources.   Website: mentalhealth.gov

National Institute of Mental Health (NIMH): NIMH is a leading research organization dedicated to understanding and treating mental illnesses. Their website offers valuable information and resources.   Website: nimh.nih.gov

Online Resources

bpHope: This online community provides support, information, and resources for people with bipolar disorder and their loved ones.   Website: bphope.com

The Mighty: This online platform allows people to share their stories, connect with others, and find support for a variety of mental health conditions.   Website: themighty.com

Hotlines

Crisis Text Line: Text HOME to 741741 from anywhere in the US, anytime, about any type of crisis.

The National Suicide Prevention Lifeline: 988 (or the previous number, 1-800-273-TALK (8255)) provides confidential support for people in distress.

Therapist Finder

Psychology Today: Their "Find a Therapist" tool allows users to search for therapists by location, specialty, insurance, and other criteria. https://www.psychologytoday.com/us/therapists

GoodTherapy: This directory features therapists who have met specific quality standards and ethical guidelines.

https://www.goodtherapy.org/find-therapist.htm

TherapyDen: TherapyDen focuses on inclusivity and features a diverse range of therapists, including those specializing in specific issues or serving marginalized communities.   https://www.therapyden.com/

Zencare: Zencare provides in-depth profiles of therapists, including videos and client reviews, to help users find a good fit.   https://zencare.co/

Inclusive Therapists: This directory focuses on connecting clients with therapists who are committed to cultural competence and serving diverse populations.

https://www.inclusivetherapists.com/

Acknowledgments

First and foremost, I offer my deepest gratitude to God, who has been my source of strength and solace throughout this arduous journey. Without His divine grace and guidance, I doubt I would have emerged from the depths of despair.

To my beloved son, Adiel, thank you for your love and patience, even as you navigate your own battles with mental illness. Together, we have fought and continue to fight, side-by-side, a testament to the enduring bond between mother and son.

My mother, Janet, deserves endless appreciation for being the epitome of a loving and supportive mother. Her strength and resilience have always inspired me, and her belief in me has carried me through countless challenges.

My favorite Aunt Elsie, who has been my lifelong friend and confidante. I can talk to her about anything, and she never judges me. She is always there for me with a listening ear, a warm hug, and support.

To my baby sister, Kami, thank you for being my confidante, my shoulder to cry on, and my best friend in the world. Your understanding and compassion have been invaluable, reminding me that I am never truly alone.

My precious niece, Kamiyah, though just three years old, has been a source of immeasurable joy and strength. From the moment she was born, her infectious laughter and boundless love have given me a reason to fight, to persevere, and to witness the extraordinary person she is destined to become.

To my brothers from another mother, Demond and Claude, thank you for your presence and support. Your daily check-ins and words of encouragement have lifted my spirits and reminded me that I am loved and valued.

To my ride-or-die besties, Avonelle and Candace thank you for being my rock, my cheerleaders, and my confidante. You both believed in me even when I struggled to believe in myself, and your support has been a lifeline.

To my first true love, Sherwyn, thank you for proving that love can transcend the challenges of mental illness. Your devotion and acceptance have shown me that I am worthy of love, even amidst my struggles, thanks for being there when many ran away.

To my church family at Bethel House of Worship, thank you for providing a spiritual home where I found acceptance, solace, and a sense of belonging. Your prayers and encouragement have lifted my spirits and strengthened my faith. I am particularly grateful to Apostle Deon, Apostle Leah, Apostle Vivian, and Apostle Jemma Duncan for their spiritual guidance and support.

And finally, I extend my heartfelt gratitude to my therapist Judy, and psychiatrist, who have guided me through the darkness and helped me understand the complexities of my own mind. Your expertise, compassion, and support have been instrumental in my journey toward healing and wholeness.

To all those who have been beacons of hope along my journey, whether through a kind word, a shared smile, or a listening ear, thank you for illuminating my path and reminding me that I am not alone.

To each and every one of you, thank you from the bottom of my heart. Your presence in my life has made all the difference.